A Paisley Collection

1. Jubilee of the Paisley Provident Co-operative Society Limited
David Rowat ISBN 0-902664-73-5

2. Saint Mirin: An account of Old Houses, Old Families and Olden
Times in Paisley
David Semple ISBN 0-902664-75-1

3. The Paisley Shawl
Matthew Blair ISBN 0-902664-80-8

4. The Paisley Thread Industry
MatthewBlair ISBN 0-902664-91-3

5. The Abbey of Paisley
J. Cameron Lees ISBN 0-902664-86-7

6. The Lordship of Paisley
William M. Metcalfe ISBN 0-902664-88-3

7. A History of Paisley
William M. Metcalfe ISBN 0-902664-89-1

8. Poems and Songs and Correspondence of Robert Tannahill
David Semple ISBN 0-902664-90-5

The Paisley Shawl

Group taken at Glenfield, 29th May, 1856

(Key is on pages 74/75)

THE PAISLEY SHAWL

AND THE
MEN WHO PRODUCED IT

*A record of an interesting epoch
in the History of the Town*

By

MATTHEW BLAIR

*Chairman of the Incorporated Weaving, Dyeing
and Printing College of Glasgow*

Glasgow
The Grimsay Press
2004

The Grimsay Press
an imprint of
Zeticula
57 St Vincent Crescent
Glasgow
G3 8NQ

http://www.thegrimsaypress.co.uk
admin@thegrimsaypress.co.uk

Transferred to digital printing in 2004

The plates originally printed in colour, and featured on the cover of this
edition, can also be found at
http://www.thegrimsaypress.co.uk/paisley_shawl/page_01.htm

Copyright © Zeticula 2004

First published in Great Britain by Alexander Gardner, Paisley in 1904

ISBN 0 902664 80 8

Reproduced from the copy in the Library of the University of Paisley,
Scotland

TO THE

MEMORY OF THOSE GRAND OLD

Paisley Weavers

WHO WERE THE FRIENDS AND INSTRUCTORS OF MY YOUTH

I Dedicate

WITH FEELINGS OF AFFECTION AND REVERENCE

These Memorials

OF AN ILLUSTRIOUS PERIOD IN THE HISTORY OF

MY NATIVE TOWN

PREFACE

IN January, 1901, the Governors of the Incorporated Weaving, Dyeing, and Printing College of Glasgow organized a Special Loan Exhibition of Paisley Shawls and similar fabrics, principally for the instruction of their students. These exquisite productions are now neither worn nor manufactured here, but many are cherished as heir-looms in families in the West of Scotland and elsewhere. One of the last acts of Her Majesty Queen Victoria was to direct two beautiful specimens to be sent to this Exhibition, thus renewing that interest which, particularly in its darkest days, Her Majesty had always taken in the Paisley Shawl Trade.

The Exhibition attracted much attention because of the artistic beauty of the shawls, and the high degree of technical skill and patient care on the part of the weavers which they exhibited. Among the visitors were many artists, some of whom came from the large industrial centres of England. At the time a very general desire was expressed that some more permanent exhibition of these beautiful fabrics should be placed in one of the local museums.

A hope was also entertained that some account of this industry might be written, as the period in the history of the town in which it was carried on was one of singular interest, not only on account of the merit of the articles produced, and the high talent shown in their manufacture, but for the marked influence which the conditions of the employment had upon the character of the workpeople engaged in it.

The writer was urged by friends to undertake this task. Brought up in the trade, he entered business life at the time when the industry began to decline. He thus witnessed the decay and extinction of the Paisley Shawl trade; and because of the consequent distress and lack of employment, had, like many other Paisley boys of that period, to go elsewhere to earn a living. Returning after an absence of more than forty years, he finds everything changed. The weavers are almost extinct. Not a draw-loom exists in the town. The very memory of the shawl trade is well-nigh lost. The present generation is engaged on other and more varied occupations, and, perhaps in consequence, the town has become one of the most prosperous in the kingdom.

The epoch of the Shawl Trade in Paisley is now rounded off. Like a flower it came up, blossomed, and decayed. Its history is full of honour to the town, and pregnant with lessons that should never be forgotten.

These pages are written with the desire to keep alive an interest in this noble past, by placing on record some description of these beautiful fabrics, as well as of the remarkable class of men who produced them, and who have now nearly all gone over to the majority.

In carrying out a task so congenial to his feelings, the writer has to acknowledge with warmest thanks the valuable assistance which he has received from Mr. John Ingram of Messrs. T. & D. Wilson & Co., of Glasgow, and Mr. Thomas Brown, Chief Instructor in the Incorporated Weaving, Dyeing, and Printing College of Glasgow, both of whom, in early life, had practical experience of the labours of the draw-boys and weavers of Paisley. He has also to express his thanks to the ladies who have so kindly allowed him to reproduce, in coloured illustrations, such beautiful examples of what has become widely known as the Paisley Shawl.

THE MOORINGS,
THORNLY PARK, PAISLEY,
    December, 1903.

CONTENTS

LIST OF ILLUSTRATIONS

THE PAISLEY SHAWL

———◆◆◆———

CHAPTER I

EARLY TEXTILES IN PAISLEY

THE textile industries of Paisley seem to have attained some importance as far back as the seventeenth century. The Poll-tax Roll of Paisley in 1695, as reproduced in Brown's *History*, shows that there were 66 weavers in the town, when the population over 16 years of age was stated to be 1,129. There were also 32 weavers in the Abbey Parish, which adjoins the burgh. This large proportion would indicate that the weavers worked for a wider market than the town or its immediate neighbourhood could afford.

The trade appears to have grown steadily :—

In 1766, there were 1,767 looms in the town.
In 1773,   ,,   2,233   ,,   ,,
In 1792,   ,,   3,602   ,,   ,,
In 1820,   ,,   7,000   ,,   ,,

The goods made in those earlier days were of home-spun linen and woollen. Burns mentions that the scanty garment of the witch in "Tam o' Shanter" was "a cutty sark o' Paisley harn." Those linen and woollen goods were, no doubt, of a plain and heavy character, but as improvements in spinning progressed, cotton and silk were added, and as the materials which he could obtain became finer and more perfect, the weaver continually advanced. Linen evolved into Lawn, Cotton into Muslin, and Silk into Gauze.

This period is commemorated in the names of the streets which were added to the town at that time. Lawn, Gauze, Incle, Cotton, Silk, and Thread Streets in the New Town, and Shuttle Street in the Old Town.

The goods were at first comparatively plain fabrics, or they were woven with checks and stripes. The next advance was to put more elaborate designs upon them. This was done in two ways. First, by sewing in a pattern by hand, called "tambouring"; so named from the two rings which hold the cloth, while the worker is sewing in the figure, having a resemblance to a drum or tambourine. The other way was, by mechanical appliances, to weave the figure into the cloth.

By the latter process, the ingenuity of the workers was developed to a marvellous extent. The weavers were in some degree their own designers, and each worked out on his loom his own ideas. The result was that they produced a great many new types of fabrics, and invented several exceedingly clever adaptations of the loom to produce novel effects.

Writing in 1872, the late Mr. William Cross, who had an intimate knowledge of those times, says :—

"The present generation, even of weavers, have little idea of the vast amount of thought and mechanical skill exercised by their predecessors in the trade on such inventions as the harness, the fly-shuttle, the patent net, the bead-lam lappet, the lappet wheel, the seeding frame, the sewing frame, the ten-box-lay, the parrot machine and the barrel machine, the 'deil,' or 'douge,' as it is sometimes called, the counterpoise motion, and the double neck. If these ingenious inventions are not soon explained, and clear descriptions of them put on record, they will utterly perish from remembrance, as if they had never been."

The hope expressed in the last sentence has not yet been realised; and we fear there is little probability that it can now be done with the necessary completeness. At best it would be of merely antiquarian interest. The power-loom has worked wonderful changes, and has superseded many of these inventions; but the harness, the lappet wheel, the sewing frame, and the box-lay, are still embodied in the power-loom of the present day.

There can be little doubt that this was the period—the close of the eighteenth century—when the weavers of Paisley acquired that intellectual culture and technical skill, for which they have been so much noted. These characteristics survived long after the sub-division of labour and the advance of mechanical appliances, had made the weaver less of an original artist than he was at first. This training also qualified him to produce with artistic skill the beautiful textures which reached their perfection in the Paisley Harness Shawl.

The Silk manufacture was introduced into Scotland about 1760, by Humphrey Fulton, who established a flourishing business in Paisley, and died in 1779. This was probably the most prosperous time in the weaving industry that Paisley ever enjoyed.

An Italian gentleman who visited the town in 1788, writes in the following glowing terms :—

"The population of Paisley interests the sensibility of a traveller, not only by the constant occupation to which he sees them devoted, but likewise by the simplicity, and, at the same time, the elegance of their manners. The town abounds with most beautiful women : these in the morning and during the day are quite retired and occupied in their trade, without shoes and stockings, as is usual over all Scotland, and poorly dressed. These same women, in summer, about eight in the evening, meet and walk through the long, neat street, which forms, as it were, the whole of the place, divided into bands, dressed with so much elegance and decency, that they invite a wish to prolong one's stay, which the Scotch vivacity, far superior to the English, promises to render agreeable and diverting. In fact, after the walk, almost every evening, there is a dance. At the hour of ten all go to sleep, and the day which succeeds is like the preceding, equally occupied, and delightful, although the town has no theatre, nor that public place, so much a favourite with the English, among whom it is common, called a bowling green, nor indeed, any other spectacle which collects and entertains the people. It is important, however, to know that this people is satisfied and completely tranquil."[1]

This is quite idyllic, and, certainly, rather highly coloured, and, we fear, could scarcely have been written after the introduction of steam and of the factory system. But, no doubt, there was another side to the picture. Some of the weavers were rollicking blades. The King Street "core," the Thread Street "core," and other "cores," were well known, and kept the neighbourhood in an uproar when they had a drinking bout. Many amusing stories are told of these worthies at times when throats were dry and finances low. Friendship was strong and deep among them. Burns paints this love in "Tam o' Shanter" :—

> "Tam lo'ed him like a verra brither ;
> They had been fou for weeks thegither."

No one but a Scot, who has witnessed such scenes, can ever grasp the intensity of the bond of brotherhood expressed in these lines.

It is satisfactory to record that these "cores" were not altogether bad. The most famous of them was the "Charleston Callans," with their big drum. Their successors still keep the name alive, although their occupation is gone. As a Benefit Society they continue to distribute assistance to the indigent in their quarter of the town, and they are not the only Society of "Callans" yet existing.

---

[1] *The Weavers' Magazine*, 1819.

Some of the weavers' wives were not behind their husbands. Scolding or "flyting" was a common failing, as appears from the records of the police courts. Such scenes as are depicted in Alexander Wilson's "Watty and Meg," written at this time, are unusual now, but were common enough then :—

> "   .   .   .   .   .   Maggie fallow'd,
>   Flyting a' the road behin.
>   Fowk frae every door came lamping,
>   Maggie curst them ane and a,'
>   Clappet wi' her hands, and, stamping,
>   Lost her bauchles i' the sna'."

Up to the beginning of the nineteenth century, nearly all the textures produced in Paisley were piece goods. The Paisley Shawl proper begins to appear then, and about 1820, the successful effort to imitate the Indian Cashmere Shawl was in full swing, and this was the culminating point of the ingenuity and skill of the weavers.

CHAPTER II

THE PAISLEY SHAWL

THE Shawl Trade of Paisley, during the time that this article of dress was in fashion, was the principal industry of the town. It was not the first class of textile woven in the district. There had previously been an extensive business in fine Muslins, in Lawns, and in certain classes of light silk goods, but these branches became quite subordinate to the manufacture of Shawls.

The Shawls were made of many classes, from the light wrap which the working-girl threw over her head before the advent of bonnets, to the warm Shepherd's Plaid, a graceful piece of attire which still maintains its popularity. But the particular shawl which afterwards became widely known as the "Paisley Shawl," was an article of what is called "harness" work. This was an attempt to produce in the loom the effects which, in the Indian Cashmere Shawl, were produced by the needle.

The Shawl came to us from the East. Mr. Cross, already quoted, says :—

"The introduction of the Shawl manufacture into this country was a result of the French Expedition to Egypt. It was from shawls sent as presents from the officers of both the European armies contending in that country, to ladies at home, that the first imitations of Turkish and Indian goods were attempted here."

Among the most beautiful products of the Eastern looms which were brought to Europe at this time, were soft woollen shawls from Cashmere, filled in with designs in needlework of a peculiar and elaborate character. Cheap as labour was in the East, these goods, by the time they reached this country, were very costly, and far beyond the reach of the ordinary buyer. These Indian Shawls were of two classes. Some of them were entirely of patchwork. A good specimen of this class is shown in Plate 2. In this shawl about 400 human figures are delineated, besides numberless bird and animal forms; the whole surrounded with rich detail work. On a close examination it will be observed that the shawl is made up of little pieces of needlework, all carefully arranged and sewn together, and probably made by many different workers. The design is exceedingly elaborate, and many years must have been spent in carrying it out. Shawls of this class, as will be observed from the example reproduced, could not be made to lie quite level or smooth, while their peculiar construction admitted of an irregularity and variety which it was impossible to imitate on the loom.

After the Patchwork Shawl comes the true Cashmere Shawl, which is a combination of needle and loom work. The weft threads, instead of being in one continuous line from side to side of the loom, are sewn in by the weaver in short lengths, the back of the fabric being to the worker. Thus, working from side to side, with several needles or small shuttles of different coloured weft in his hands, he sews in the colours along one line of weft, as required by the design, and so completes one shot, although this line of weft is broken up into many hundreds of little bits. A shawl of this class would occupy one or two weavers for several years, and the cost was proportionately high. A fine specimen of this work is represented in Plate 3. It was this class of shawl that the Paisley weavers successfully imitated on the loom. The ingenious methods and the patient labour by which they attained this end will be described further on.

The Paisley Harness Shawl attained great celebrity, and the skill of the weavers, and the enterprise of the manufacturers, maintained its supremacy against the competition of Norwich and France. In 1834, the shawls made in Paisley were estimated to be of the value of one million sterling. In the official reports of the Exhibitions of 1851 and 1862, the exhibits of the Paisley manufacturers are mentioned with special approval.

The Paisley Shawl became the universal bridal present. In Paisley, and many other places, it was the fashion for all newly-married ladies to be "kirked" in a Paisley Harness Plaid, quite irrespective of the state of the weather. This custom went out about 1870, but these bridal gifts are the cherished possessions of many families in Paisley. Plate 4 represents a shawl of this class. Ladies who could afford it, usually endeavoured to have a white or scarlet-centre shawl for summer wear, and a "filled-over" shawl for colder days. Cloaks and jackets were then for ladies practically unknown. Plate 5 represents a fine specimen of the "filled-in" class. It was manufactured by Messrs. David Speirs & Co., and awarded a medal at the Exhibition in London in 1862.

For all important functions the Paisley Shawl was considered the appropriate article of dress. During the depression of trade, in 1842, Her Majesty Queen Victoria, ever ready to sympathise with those in trouble, selected and purchased seventeen Paisley Shawls. In a letter, written from Windsor Castle by one of her secretaries to Provost Henderson, under date 21st January, 1842, it is stated that Her Majesty would wear one of them on the day of the Royal christening. This must have been the baptism of the Prince of Wales, the present King Edward.

Plate 8 represents one of these shawls, but with a differently coloured centre from the one supplied to Her Majesty, and most probably exhibits the design of the one worn by her on that occasion. It may be noted in passing that it is designed without the pine ornament.

Patch Work Indian Shawl

CHAPTER III

DESIGN OF THE PAISLEY SHAWL—THE PINE PATTERN

THE shawl is essentially an Oriental piece of dress, and in its two forms of a square and a long shawl, or scarf, called also a plaid, it still maintains its place in the East, although not now much worn in Europe. The shawls which came to this country from Egypt were of Turkish origin, and were successfully imitated by the Paisley weavers, and a considerable trade done. As the public taste began to run on this class of goods, many new varieties were produced, such as the Damask, Barege, Canton Crape, Chenille, and many other kinds of shawls. The designs of the Turkish shawls were governed by the religious ideas of the Mohammedans, which do not favour the representation of living creatures. They were mainly geometrical, of a somewhat unnatural and fantastic character.

The imitation Turkish shawl, however, was only a stepping stone to the real Paisley Shawl, which came in about 1820. In it the style of art is a blending of Hindoo and Arab ideas. The Mohammedan invaders of India penetrated as far down the valley of the Ganges as Benares, but the chief cities of the Mogul Empire were Agra and Delhi. The art of the period, still preserved in the public buildings of these cities, affords abundant evidence of this blending of Hindoo

27

and Arab ideas. It is seen also in the designs of the Cashmere shawls. These shawls were all the product of the needle upon a fine woollen ground. The colours in nearly every case were primary. Few secondary tints were admitted, the effect being rather in the direction of jewellery, or barbaric gem work. The designs were modified by the European manufacturers, but the leading types were preserved. The most characteristic of these was the pine pattern. This graceful ornament was present in one form or another in almost every real Cashmere shawl, and no imitation of these goods was considered true to art which did not include the design of the pine. The manufacturers occasionally introduced other forms, but these were never popular with the public; and the pine always remained the characteristic feature of the Paisley Shawl.

Several explanations of the origin and meaning of this design have been advanced. It has a certain resemblance to the fruit of the mango tree, and in some parts of India designs in which the pine is a feature are called the mango pattern, hence it has been supposed to be derived from the shape of the mango fruit. But the true origin and signification of the pine form in art has been fully explained by Sir George C. M. Birdwood, M.D., K.C.I.E.[1] The subject has since been further developed by Count Goblet D'Alviella, and by other eminent writers at home and abroad.[2]

[1] *Industrial Arts of India*, p. 325.
[2] *La Migration du Symbol*, p. 175. Paris: 1891.

Indian Cashmere Shawl

The pine is a conventionalised form of a religious symbol. It originated in Chaldea, from whence it spread into India on the one hand, and to Europe on the other. In Chaldea the date palm was a first necessity of existence, and hence came to be used as the symbol of the fertility of nature in supplying food. It was known as the Tree of Life, and is intimately connected with ancient worship. Two ornaments were derived from it, and were constantly used in religious decoration (*see* Plate 10):

(1) The pine or cone, which was the male or pollen-bearing inflorescence of the date palm, and hence symbolic of the renewal and communication of life. Associated with the flower, it thus became a symbol of the Creator, and as such was, and is still, venerated in the East. It was constantly employed in worship, and is present as an ornament in the religions of Persia, Egypt, and Palestine. The pine and its flower are in reality the knop and flower ornaments used in the Tabernacle in the wilderness (Exodus, xxv. 31). The same sacred symbol of the Creator was repeated in the decorations of Solomon's Temple (I. Kings, vi. 18).[1]

(2) The foliage of the date palm gave rise to what is called the "honeysuckle ornament," so well known in Greek art.[2]

It is thus easy to understand how the pine as a form of decoration came to be so generally employed in Indian art. The

[1] Introduction to the English translation of *La Migration du Symbol*, p. 14.
[2] *The Industrial Arts of India*, p. 334.

Hindoo is essentially a religious man, and a mystic. Religion, in form at least, colours all his life, and affects his art. He is continually symbolizing ideas, and incarnating the attributes of his gods, and, as the Indian craftsman was in most cases his own designer, he worked in with the needle the symbolic forms of the ideas which governed his life.

The pine form, signifying fertility, reproduction, abundance, was thus continually introduced into decorative work, whether sacred or secular. Through time it became more and more conventionalised and more varied in form. Frequently a large pine was made up of a number of small pines, and wreathed with floral sprays. Some of the shawls were entirely covered with the design. Others had it as a border, with the centre of a different colour, into which occasionally the design strayed, producing very beautiful effects. Plates 4, 5, 6, 7, 8, and 9 are representations of these different classes.

The religious signification, however, was not the cause of the European preference for the pine pattern. It had been universally present in all real Indian shawls, and was a form graceful and agreeable to the eye, and is still popular in printed and woven fabrics.

As an article of dress, the shawl went out of fashion about 1870. Parisian influence is too strong for the fair sex, none of whom would now care to appear in the somewhat stiff and formal dress required to show the beauty of the Paisley Shawl. Nevertheless, these relics of a bygone time are lovingly preserved in many a family in Paisley, and in other towns and in other lands, and although never worn, are highly valued and admired.

Notwithstanding that the shawl, and more particularly the Paisley Shawl, has long disappeared from Central Europe, it still lingers on the outskirts, in countries not much given to change.

In Norway, the wives of the peasants don the ancient Paisley Shawl on Sundays; and in soft Andalusia, at the opposite end of Europe, many a señora still promenades of an afternoon on the all enjoyable Alameda, or goes to a bull fight attired in a harness shawl, worn with the coquettish grace peculiar to those daughters of the sun. Some of these shawls may be of Paisley origin, and of old date. Perhaps some may still be made in France, but the manufacture of them has now ceased in this country.

CHAPTER IV

PREPARATION OF THE LOOM

IF the reader be a weaver, he will forgive the attempt to make so technical a subject intelligible, and if not a weaver, he will at least be enabled to form some idea of the skill and patience exhibited by the harness weavers. To the ordinary reader it may be necessary to explain that the weaving of a piece of cloth with a continuous pattern, however elaborate, which goes on repeating itself, is a comparatively simple matter. Any irregularity of thickness in the weaving, while it will be a defect, will not entirely destroy the symmetry of the pattern. But it is quite otherwise with a shawl, which has a beginning and an end. The weaver commences to weave a border across the bottom, which in some measure repeats itself along the sides, and blends into a border across the opposite end. To produce the design correctly, a fixed number of weft threads must be woven across, between the beginning and the end; not one more, and not one less. It is manifest that if the weaver beats up his weft threads too closely at the beginning, he will have the total number in before he arrives at the end of the shawl, and where, as is often the case, the warp is dyed or stained in portions to correspond with the design, the latter part of the pattern will be wholly destroyed. In a power-loom the exact number of weft threads in a given

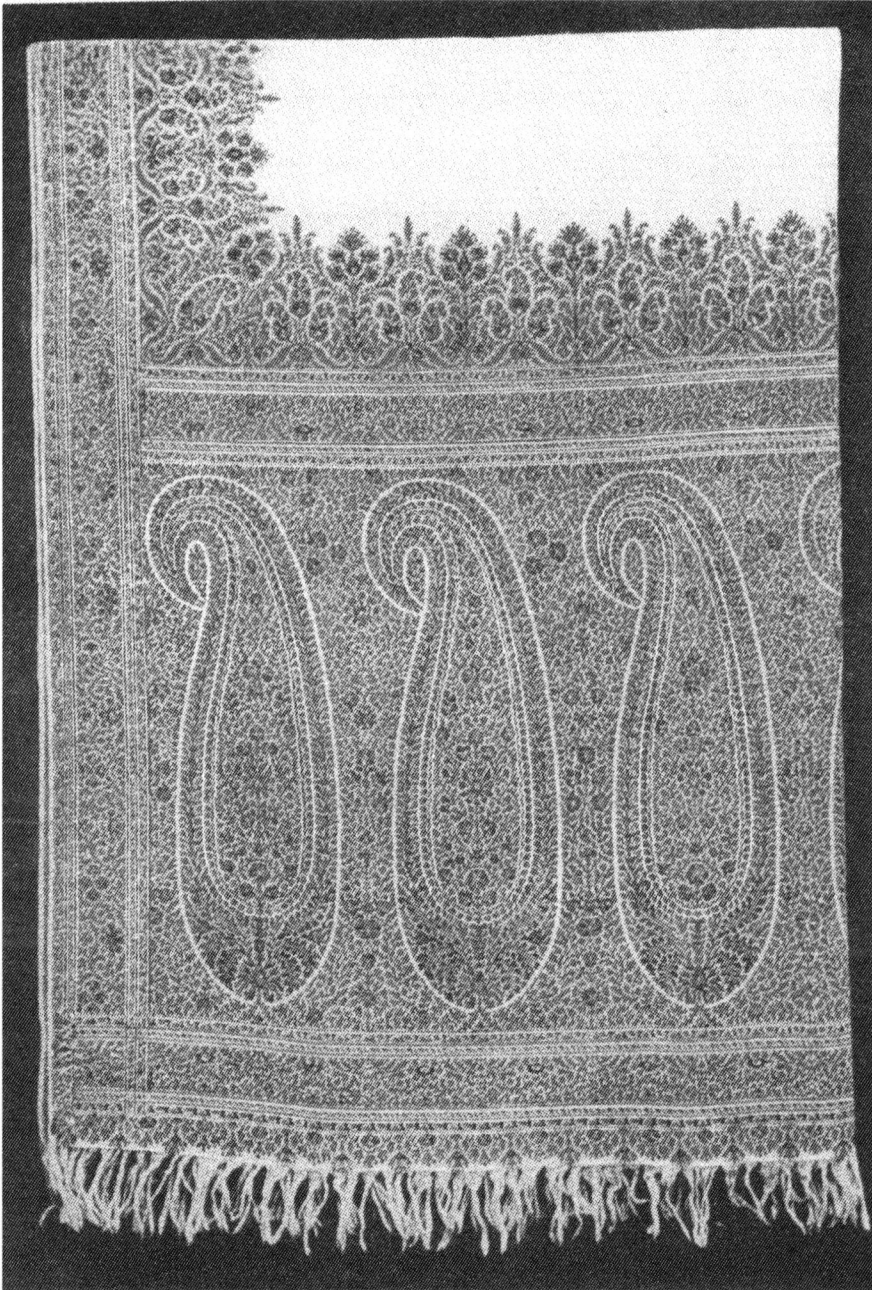

Paisley Shawl, White Centre

space can be regulated with absolute accuracy, but the hand-loom weaver had to trust to the delicacy of his touch, and therein lay much of the skill of the harness weaver.

The yarn required for these Harness Shawls had to be specially prepared. The finest class of it went under the name of Cashmere. To give the strength necessary for warp, it consisted of a thread of fine silk round which was spun a coating of the finest Cashmere wool. This class of yarn was most successfully made in the neighbourhood of Amiens, in France, and is still manufactured there for the French market. For the less expensive qualities a silk or cotton warp was used. The weft was either a carded woollen yarn or a Botany worsted. These classes of yarn were spun principally in Yorkshire. There being no railways in those days, some of the spinners in the Bradford district were accustomed to ride down to Paisley, a journey of several days, with their yarn samples in their saddle-bags. The goods were sent round by the steamer from Liverpool to the Clyde.

The dyeing of the warps was one of the first anxieties of the manufacturers, and required great skill and care. This arose from the custom, as in the Eastern originals, of having at each end of the shawl a parti-coloured finish, showing bands of four or five different colours, which became the ground-work of the terminal borders and formed the warp fringe. This will be seen in several of the Plates. Between these parti-coloured ends the centre would be dyed red, if for a red-centered shawl, or black, if this was to be the colour of the centre. In some cases the

3

warp for the side borders might be dyed a special colour.   It
is obvious that this further necessitated much care in the warp-
ing of the web, each length and space requiring exact measure-
ment and marking.   The dyer screwed down the slides of a
frame at these marks, leaving exposed the particular piece
that was to be dyed, which was then dipped in the dye vat.
This might occur many times throughout the length of the
shawl.   The art of Dyeing thus came to great perfection in
Paisley.   While on this subject, it is also worthy to note that,
some years ago, the dyeing of piece goods made of wool or
worsted was confined to Yorkshire.   Paisley has since taken a
high place in this important industry, and for this the town is
largely indebted to the enterprise of Messrs. William Fulton &
Sons, of Glenfield.   Many of the leading dyers in Scotland and
England received their early training in Paisley.

Having now the warp ready, the next thing was to set up the
loom.   This was a work of much labour, requiring care and skill
in every detail.   Two or three weeks were often required to equip
a loom for an expensive plaid.   The weaver bore the cost of this,
but a fine spirit of comradeship prevailed, and willing help at the
tyeing of the harness was freely given by the shop-mates, who in
turn received like help when their time of need came.   The boys
employed in the weaving-shops also assisted, and were rewarded
by a feast of bread and cheese, which in those days was a great
treat to them, while to their seniors was added the inevitable dram.

On the manufacturer's part the first important point was, of course, the selection of the design. This was always shown in a miniature form—the sketch being often a work of art, fit to be framed for wall decoration (*see* Plate 11). The next step was to transfer this sketch to design or point paper, which, when completed, might in some cases cover the floor space of a good-sized room. This designing required minute care. Each small square must bear its own colour; no blurring was allowable (*see* Plate 12).

This design or point paper was first made in Paisley by Mr. Andrew Blaikie, Engraver, and was printed directly from the copper or steel plates engraved by himself, some of which are still in use by his successors, Messrs. Robert Hay & Son.

The squares represented the point at which a weft thread crossed a warp thread, so that every weft shot that was to complete the shawl could be counted, and there would be sometimes as many as 150,000 weft threads crossing the loom in one harness plaid.

If Paisley Shawls were now manufactured, the next step would be the card cutting of the design. But in those early days the Jacquard, although long before invented, was not in use by the Paisley weavers, and instead of the card cutter, the work of the flower lasher came into play, which we may now attempt to describe.

The composition of the design was usually limited to six, seven, or eight colours, and the ground colour upon which these figuring colours were introduced. The first point was to determine the sequence in which these colours would run, say: 1, claret; 2, green; 3, yellow; 4, blue; and so on.

The flower lasher had before him a frame not unlike that of a card cutter, but in addition, an upright web of strong linen thread called a "simple." This is illustrated in Plate 12. The simple was fixed tight before the lasher, each thread standing before each upright square of the design. A straight-edge placed across the design revealed only one minute horizontal line of colour. The lasher had at his left hand a bobbin of strong cotton thread, and running his eye from left to right, if claret covers two squares, he interlaces the cotton thread behind the corresponding threads of the simple, and so on across the face of the design. This is now knotted up and called a "lash." The next colour, green, is treated in like manner, and so on, till all the colours are gone over, and when completed they form a "bridle." Each lash represented one colour, and each bridle the whole of the colours in one line of weft. The twines of the simple were attached overhead to the tail cords, which were passed over pulleys and connected with the harness twines. At the lower end of each of these harness twines was a metal eye, called a "mail," through which the warp thread passed, with a weight below in the form of a thin piece of lead, to bring it down and keep it straight. *See* Plate 13.

It was the manipulation of these lashes on the simple that formed the work of the draw-boy. Drawing out each lash in succession, the boy grasped the threads of the simple, thus separating them from the others, and pulled them down, so raising the requisite warp threads to form the shed through which the shuttle passed.

Paisley Shawl, Filled

CHAPTER V

WEAVING OF THE HARNESS SHAWL

THE shawl was woven face downwards. To the weaver there appeared only a mass of floating threads, without form and void. Close attention on the part both of weaver and draw-boy was thus necessary every moment, in order to prevent any false shot from passing in to mar the design.

The weaver had another constant care before him. Every inch that he wove must measure to the minutest fraction, neither more nor less, than the precise space allotted by the design. This perfect accuracy arose because of the necessity that a plaid of three or four yards in length must terminate within a quarter of an inch of its stipulated length. The former reference to the mode of dyeing or staining the warps will make this obvious.

How much skill and delicacy of touch was required will be plain to every reader. As an aid to guide him, the weaver usually passed a pin through the cloth, and carefully measured each three or four inches, knowing, as he did, that 100 or a 1,000 shots ought to measure a definite length, or complete so much of the design. And it must be acknowledged to be a triumph of weaving, that in a plaid measuring three or four yards in length, with six or seven colours running, and a heavy box-lay to handle, the plaid should be brought to a perfect finish within a quarter of an inch of its assigned limit.

The lay in common use was one of ten boxes, with a drop motion controlled by a trigger under the weaver's thumb, so that he could raise or drop each box in succession, or skip one or more as required. Thus, if eight colours formed the design, it might happen that colour 3 in the gamut of colours was silent in a particular bridle. The draw-boy would see this by a gap being left, and call out "miss ane;" the weaver would then drop box 3 and pass to the fourth colour. When the completed shots of each bridle had passed through, then would follow the ground shot; but as this was often a heavy lift, too much for a boy to raise, he had the control of a strong wooden lever, moving on a spindle, called the "deil" or "douge." Pressing this against the simple, the heavy lift was thus made, and the ground shots were passed through.

The ground colour of the fabric was generally fine Thibet wool (Botany worsted), and being of a smaller count or thinner thread than the spotting or figure colours, there were usually two or more shots put in for one of the spotting colours, the threads of which were always thicker. The bridle was therefore composed of, say two ground shots, one of each of the spotting colours, and then a shot of fine lace cotton. This is the "sma' shot" which is commemorated in the holiday, as explained further on. The small shot acted as a binder for all the other colours, and was not intended to be seen. It was put through a shed formed by the weaver with heddles continuous across the width of the warp, and not by any action of the draw-boy. The ground or back lash was formed by the boy drawing out all the lashes of a bridle with the left hand and passing in the "deil" with the right hand. Pushing it back with all that remained of the simple, he raised the ground shed, which had to be held up for two shots, the weaver forming the twill by treading the heddles.

It was arduous work for a young boy, requiring continuous attention, as a mistake on his part might work havoc on the design. Like his master, he too needed a careful touch. Lash number 1 might represent only a few threads of the simple, and so a light touch was needed to make the required shed. Lash number 5 might need all his strength to draw it down and so make a clear passage for the shuttle. If the weaver were harsh and exacting, the poor boy was in constant fear lest a slip might be made. But even under a kindly master, the work was heavy, and often the hours were long, running sometimes near to midnight on occasional emergencies. In cold weather his bare feet would be nestled within his Kilmarnock bonnet, resting on the clay floor. And yet these boys were a brave cheery race, full of fun and mischief, and ready for any ploy when the web was out, or the "maister" gone for a day to the fishing or curling, or mayhap on the "spree." Indeed, the draw-boys rather preferred a master who occasionally enjoyed himself "not wisely but too well." Not a few of these draw-boys rose to positions of influence in the old

country, and in the " Greater Britain " beyond the seas.   Peace
be to their memory.

In the way we have endeavoured to describe, the old weavers
made beautiful and perfect productions.   It would be difficult
now to find handicraft workers to exhibit such patience, skill, and
devotion.   It was severe work, both for man and boy.   Verily
the workers of our day have a lighter lot to face.   But these old
weavers had some compensations.   Out of the travail of this
drudgery, was born the patient industry, the intellectual strength,
the cultured taste, and that love of beauty in fabrics, in nature,
and in song, which marked the weavers of Paisley.

Although the weaving of the Harness Shawl was a delicate
operation, and had a highly educative effect on the workman,
there were many preparatory and subsidiary occupations connected
with the shawl manufacture, where highly skilled labour was also
required.   No weaver, however wide his knowledge and experi-
ence, could undertake the whole of these operations, and thus
specialists arose for every department.   This was an important
point in the spread of the very high intellectual training, which
the Harness Shawl trade, above many other occupations, was
instrumental in promoting.

The designing was a very special department, and demanded
a wide culture.   Designing for a garment that is to be draped on
the figure, differs materially from that destined for a wall-paper or
a carpet.   A good shawl designer had not only to be a careful
student of Indian art, and of design in general, he had also to

Paisley Shawl, Red Centre

understand the limits which a loom imposes on design, and to know the number of warp threads which the harness could control, and so construct his pattern that it would be possible to produce it on the loom that then existed, and at a price that would command the market. Thus the designers requiring in addition to their artistic skill, to possess considerable technical knowledge, were quite a superior class of operatives.

Dyeing was equally important, and required highly skilled workmen. From the necessity of having the parti-coloured finish on the border, and different coloured portions through all the length of the warp, dyeing became practically a system of printing, and had to be most carefully done. Men were thus trained in handicraft to a degree of skill, and with an intelligence that has very little counterpart in many of our present industries. To enable the dyer to properly stain or print the warp, the warping had to be so carefully done as to create another class of specialists known as warpers. The kind of work to which these men devoted themselves required the utmost delicacy. One of the most exacting parts of the manufacturer's duty was the drawing of the dyeing plan, so as to guide correctly both the warpers and the dyers.

The placing of such a stained warp on the beam ready for the weaver, was the work of the beamers, and this also required a specially trained class of men, who entirely devoted themselves to this operation. The stained portions had to be placed accurately at their proper place. Certain little flaws might be afterwards remedied with a paint brush, but any material error in the beaming would produce a damaged plaid, hence this important operation came to be a special industry.

Designing, warping, staining, and beaming were operations outside of the loom, and none of the weavers undertook any part of these operations. But in the loom, the harness-tying and the entering were occasionally done by the weaver himself, if he were competent, but in most cases these matters were confided to specialists. Harness-tiers thus became a separate class of operatives, who had great skill in this work and could do it much quicker than any weaver. Entering the web, that is, passing each thread through its proper eye in the mail or heddle, became a distinct profession of the enterers, who were much more expert at this delicate and responsible operation than any weaver could be.

The work of the flower-lasher, also, formed a separate profession. This subdivision of labour not only produced the best work, but it widely extended the culture of the operatives.

Even when the shawl came out of the loom, it had to go to professional clippers, to clear the under part of the loose threads, a work that had to be confided to specially trained hands. The clipping machine was a framework carrying a set of steel blades, which revolved at a great speed, under which the shawl was passed several times, each closer than the preceding, till all the loose threads were cleanly shaven off. The weight of the shawl would thus sometimes be reduced from one hundred ounces, when it came out of the loom, to thirty four ounces, which was considered the average weight for a good quality of plaid. It is evident that this operation, although done by a machine, required an intelligent and skilful worker. The slightest error in the adjustment of the knives might destroy a valuable plaid.

Then followed the fringing, finishing, and pressing of the shawls, which again employed people specially trained to these matters. Thus all the workers connected with the manufacture of the shawl had to be intelligent, patient, and skilful. The work in all its branches contributed to form that cultured character which marked the Paisley operative.

The Paisley Shawl as now described, was woven on the draw-loom by the aid of the draw-boy. The mechanism of this loom is shown in Plate 13.

Attempts were made as far back as 1728 to do the draw-boy's work by means of perforated cards. This invention was perfected by a French weaver, Joseph Marie Jacquard (1752-1834), in the machine which bears his name, and which was first shown in 1801. The French adopted it much earlier than the Paisley weavers. Ultimately it made its way here, and gradually superseded the draw-boy, who was rarely employed after 1850.

Mechanical improvements of this kind were inevitable and desirable, yet the tendency of machinery is to alter entirely the type of workman, and thus the old cultured and ingenious weaver gradually disappeared.

Before leaving this subject, it may be well to mention the introduction of the double or reversible shawl. The harness shawl, as we have said, was woven face downwards, and the loose threads at the back were cut off by a clipping machine, so that the pattern was shown only on one side. In the reversible shawl, the warp and weft threads were so arranged as to show a pattern on both sides, and no loose ends required to be cut off. Mr. John Cunningham was principally concerned in this invention. Plate 9 shows a shawl of this class. It will be observed that the part folded over, is the same design as the lower portion, but with the colours reversed.

Large numbers of reversible shawls were made between 1860 and 1885, but the invention came too late to give the inventor the reward which his ingenuity deserved. The shawl as an article of dress went out of fashion, and no improvements or cheapening of production, could revive the demand. Even if fashion had not changed, the hand-loom industry, which had so much to do with the development of the peculiar character of the weavers of Paisley, was certain to decay, in face of the general adoption of the power-loom. The great mass of the public will always purchase in the end, the machine-made article because of its cheapness.

Paisley Shawl, black centre

CHAPTER VI

CULTURE AND SKILL OF THE WEAVERS

THE age of handicraft is passing away. The steam-engine has worked the greatest revolution that has ever taken place in the affairs of men, and marks a dividing line between the old and the new states of society, more sharply than any other event has done. Before the application of steam power became general, hand labour held the field, and the economic conditions were such, that men could thrive simply by manual labour. But steam has put an end to all that. Power being now available, the invention of labour-saving machinery has so lessened the cost of articles of primary necessity, that hand labour cannot successfully compete.

We must, of course, accept the condition and changes which the advance of civilization imposes upon us. Our duty is to conform to them and utilize them to the best advantage. Yet it may be permissible to note with regret the deterioration in the character of the workman, which the adoption of machinery and the factory system, in their early stages, at least, have produced. We cannot go back to hand labour, but the problem of the future will be, how to counteract the demoralizing effect of machinery on our working population. Handicraft is an education. The hand worker has scope to exercise taste, invention, harmony, art, and genius, in a way that the worker who simply tends a machine can never have. He has therefore opportunities of being a far more cultured man; and this is well illustrated in the weavers of Paisley. The work they had to do required great nicety of touch, patient skill and devotion, and was thus in itself an education. The result was to produce workmen who, for general intelligence, have no counterpart at the present day. We have heard it remarked by a well informed bookseller, that many of the weavers of those days had libraries equal to those of ministers or professional men.

Some occupations are so noisy that an operative cannot think while they are being carried on. Others require a great amount of muscular exertion in circumstances most unfavourable for thought or reflection, such as blacksmiths or miners. Others again require to be performed by a number of men at one time, working into each others' hands, so that one cannot stop unless they all stop. Others, as baking and moulding, require to go on when once started, otherwise the material is spoiled. But hand-loom weaving, as practised in Paisley at the time of which we are now writing, had not one of these disadvantages, but had many peculiar advantages which rendered it especially favourable to intellectual development.

The population had not increased then as it has done since the introduction of the Irish element, brought about by the Irish famine and the making of our railways. The people were native Scotch. The parochial school system was sufficient to overtake the wants of the population, and in the country districts, at all events, even the humblest were sure of a fair education. Any one who reads the letters of Burns will see that he, educated at a parish school, could write as good English prose as any peer's son who had spent the best years of his life at Oxford or Cambridge. The lads, therefore, who flocked in from the country to learn the art of weaving, brought with them the elements of a fair education. The work they had to do was indoors. It was not very noisy. It was not pressingly continuous. It was even to some extent mechanical, and left the mind and the tongue free to exercise themselves even in the midst of the operation. Yet it was not an uninteresting labour. The setting up of the web and the handling of the delicate materials then used, required nicety and skill, and gave scope for much ingenuity. The brain was not allowed to slumber, and the eye was educated by dealing with brilliant and harmonious colours and elegant designs.

Then the work was not conducted in a factory, where a man is merely a unit, nor in a private house, where he is alone. The system of "shops," where four or six looms were set up in the same apartment, brought the weavers into constant contact with each other, so that, as of old, "As iron sharpeneth iron, so a man sharpeneth the countenance of his friend." At meal times, and before resuming their work, the weavers would gather round the fire, or on bright days, at the front door, to smoke and talk. Of course they must argue. The man who would not differ from his neighbour, and show good reasons for so doing, was no true

Paisley weaver. Newspapers were expensive in those days, but the weaver would want many things before he would do without his paper, so they usually combined to purchase a weekly journal. Generally one was set up to read to the others, and so the well-worn copy of the *Reformers' Gazette*, or the *Glasgow Chronicle*, went the round of the shops. When the time was up, the weavers went back to their "seat-trees" to ruminate on the knotty points, and prepare for another debate on the earliest opportunity.

Then, again, the work was paid by the piece, and not by time. The weaver generally owned the loom at which he worked, or hired it for a lengthy period. He was thus his own master. If the weather was fine, and the woods and meadows inviting, he could enjoy himself as he pleased, and make it up by overtime. After his web was set up, each man could work quite independently of his neighbour. If then a weaver were behind with his work, he had only to light his candle or "crusie," and go down to the shop—they mostly lived over the shops—and drive away at his loom as far into the night as he desired to work, if he had a plain web which did not require the help of a draw-boy.

Thus the weaver was delightfully self-contained and independent. He could lay down his shuttle at any moment, and take it up again when it suited him, and neither he nor his web was any the worse. All the conditions of his work and his surroundings were favourable to intellectual development.

Paisley Shawl, blue and white

CHAPTER VII

INFLUENCE OF THE TOWN AND SURROUNDINGS

PAISLEY was not a large town, nor a rich town, nor a town of noisy traffic and movement. There were few of those temptations to vice and dissipation, that are presented in all large cities. The terrible squalor and wickedness, which, alas, seem to follow everywhere the steps of wealth, and hang like a retribution upon it, were little observable in Paisley. Neither would one meet with the allurements, the flaunting vice, and the coarse manners of a seaport town. Paisley streets were quiet and uninviting. The population was employed indoors. But if the town had few temptations, the neighbourhood had many attractions. All around, Nature presented herself in some of her loveliest forms. There were the Gleniffer Braes, the Birks o' Stanley Shaw, the Bonnie Woods of Craigielea, with their dark waving plantings, their flowery leas, their milk-white thorns, and whinny knowes.

In a few minutes' walk, the weaver could be beyond the sound of the shuttle and the voice of man, and in presence of all the attractions of the country. No wonder, then, that these sweet influences awoke the poetical feeling, and that Paisley produced a long roll of minor poets, who

> "Sang amid the shuttles' din,
> The music of the woods."

4

So much was this the case, that it was a common saying at that time, that in Paisley every third man you met was a poet. We may at least say that the poetic instinct was widely spread in the town. It is noticeable about all these Paisley poets, that they avoid dealing with the sterner passions, or of depicting tragic scenes. The sublime they never attempt, nor the heroic. There is nothing of Byron or of Milton about them. Their models are to be found in Allan Ramsay's "Gentle Shepherd," or in some of the sweeter lyrics of Burns. They excel in painting natural scenes and quiet domestic life and love. There can be no doubt that the influence of Burns was very great upon the weavers at this period. The freshness and vigour of his poems, the wit and humour, and the delightful descriptions of nature, made them very attractive. The weavers also were better able than some of us now are, to understand the language used by Burns, much of which has since fallen out of use.

Robert Tannahill was the most celebrated of those weaver poets. His writings, although lacking the fire and force of Burns, are models of purity and sweetness, and his songs, many of which were set to music by his friend, R. A. Smith, who was precentor of the Abbey Church at that time, have long been much admired. Many of the weavers were good musicians, and glee and quartette parties were numerous, and their long winter evenings were often enlivened with agreeable melody. Others of them took to the cultivation of natural science. They were great in collections of birds' eggs, and they were bird fanciers to a man. Canaries,

larks, and mavises, were in every house, or their cages were hung
near the looms, to enliven the weavers at their work. Alexander
Wilson, the ornithologist, was a product of this taste.

Botany was also a favourite study, and many of the weavers
attained considerable proficiency in this science. Floriculture
was successfully followed in their little gardens. The Paisley
Florist Society has existed since 1782. Entomology was another
of their studies, and not a few of the collections in natural science
which enrich our local museum, are the results of the labours of
those early Paisley weavers. Fishing was also one of their
recreations, and the practice of the "gentle art," accorded well
with their love of poetry and of nature. Many were the happy
days they spent where—

"'Neath the brae the burnie jouks."

They were provident too, these thrifty men. The Old Weavers'
Society was incorporated in 1702, and is one of the oldest benefit
societies in the country.

It is to be noted specially, that the tastes of the weavers were
generally for recreations of a quiet and meditative nature.
Perhaps the sedentary character of their occupation indisposed
them for violent exercises. Certain it is, that although there was
a racecourse in Paisley, and a set of Silver Bells given as a prize
by the Corporation since 1620, the weavers were not at all
"horsey." They might go with the crowd, mostly composed of
Glasgow visitors, to the Saint James' Day Races, but no one ever
heard of a weaver ruining himself on the turf. Horse racing and

betting were somewhat out of their line. You might more readily find them taking a stroll round the racecourse grounds, or wandering in the Moss woods, than greatly interested as to who should win the Silver Bells.

They enjoyed a game at bowls on some of the numerous Paisley greens, or on the one at the Renfrew Ferry, and it was a group of these quiet men, wandering down by the banks of the Cart to the "Water Neb," who founded the famous "Potato and Herring Incorporation," the annual festival of which at Renfrew, instituted in 1798, is still celebrated on the Wednesday nearest the September full moon, so that the diners might safely see their way home to Paisley.

The only sport of an active character to which the weavers were addicted, was the national game of curling. When the frost was keen, and likely to hold, then would the shuttle be thrown down, and not a web finished in Paisley for weeks. Then would the "roaring game" be in full swing, and "soop it up, soop it up," be heard from morn to eve, on the glittering lochs and ponds. Then would the "beef and greens," be reeking rarely on the groaning table of many a cosy "houff," to be followed by song and chatter over the tumblers of steaming toddy. Then would the "cork" forget his dignity for a time, and the minister, the weaver, the laird, and the bailie, be bosom friends—as long as the frost lasted.

These were the days when men were happily ignorant of railways and telegraphs. They were content to take time to live,

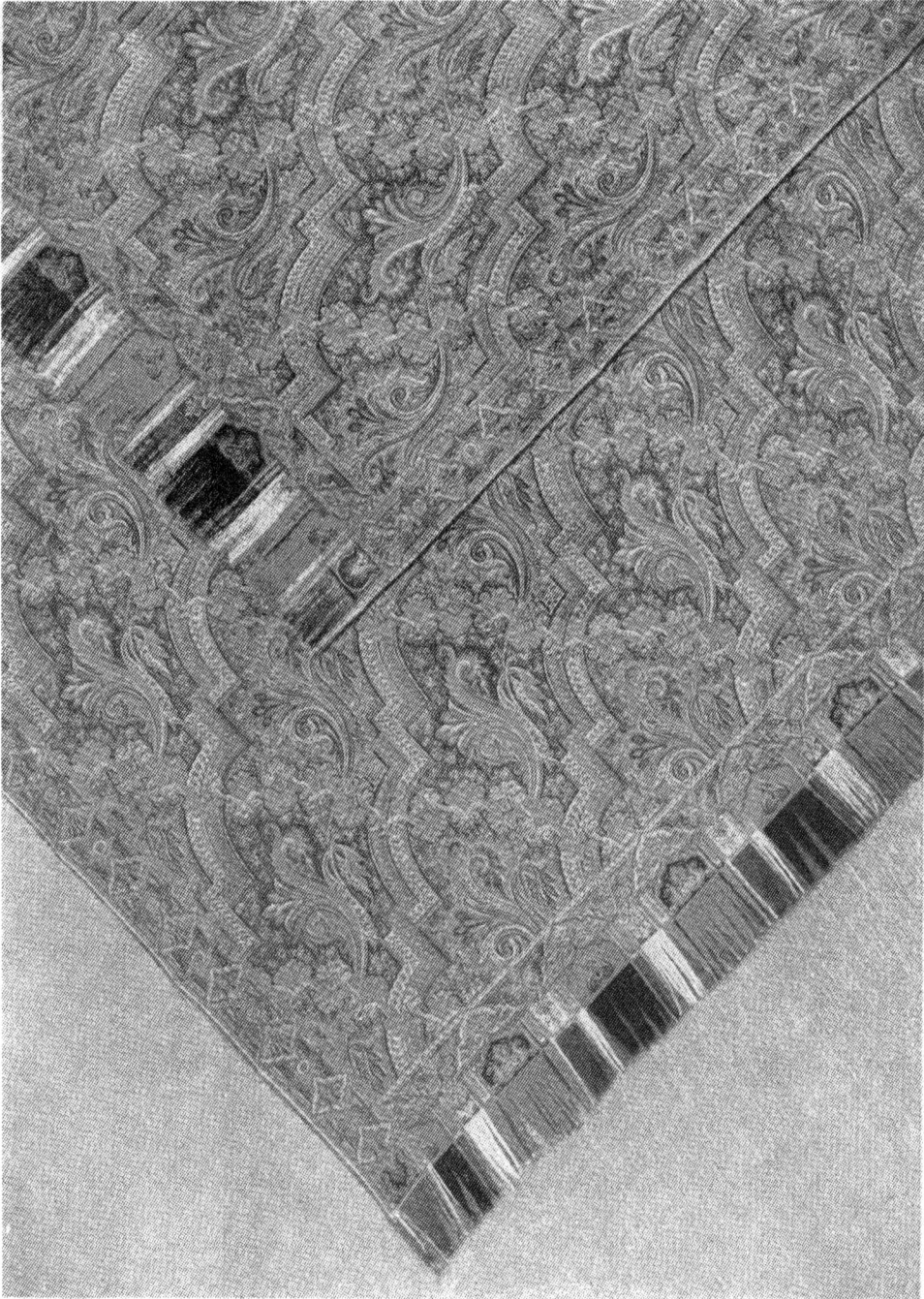

Reversible Shawl

and were perhaps better able to learn the noble lesson of human brotherhood.

Many of the weavers' wives were not behind their husbands in intelligence. They were more noted, however, for sound practical sense and good household management. None of them ever aspired to be poets or politicians, and women's suffrage was unheard of then. They seem to have thought that one genius in a family was enough. If John was to busy himself with the affairs of the nation, Jeanie must attend to the affairs of the house, and many a family was brought up in comfort, mainly by the thrift and capacity of the mother. The younger women found ample employment in winding the yarn, in fringing and hemming the shawls, in preparing the details of the harness, and in tambouring.

CHAPTER VIII

THE DRAW-BOYS

EVERY Paisley boy, no matter of what station in life, was sure to have a relative who was a harness weaver, and it was one of the delights of his life to be sent on an errand to these friends. Perhaps it would be to a low, thatched cottage in Maxwellton or Lylesland, or to a more pretentious two-storey house in Castle Street or Charleston. If it happened to be the time of the four o'clock smoke, the weavers would be seen lounging at the close mouth, with their hands under their white aprons, the pipe in the cheek, bauchles on the feet, and a red worsted night-cap on the head. Debate was sure to be in full swing, and one more dogmatic than the rest would be laying down the law to the circle of admiring and contentious shop-mates. This was a time that they enjoyed.

In the periods of depression many of the weavers emigrated to the Colonies. A gentleman travelling in Canada stopped at a tidy and prosperous looking farm-steading, and finding that the occupant had been a Paisley weaver, asked how he liked his new life. The reply was that he had plenty, but he sadly missed the " crack at the close mouth ! "

54

But however absorbed in debate the weaver might be, the young visitor would be received with a kindly smile and a pat on the head, for the weavers were fond of the bairns, and always made them welcome. There, on the ground floor, would be the four or six-loomed shop, with its clean, bright windows, for the care of the windows opposite a harness loom was confided to the draw-boy, and there was often great emulation among them as to who should have the cleanest windows. The same care, however, did not extend to the fire-place, which was beneath the dignity of a draw-boy, and was always untidy, save in shops where there was a *female* "draw-boy" employed, as was not infrequently the case. Then the fire-place was a model of tidiness, for Maggie could never "thole" the sight of a dirty fireside. Would that all the wives of our working-men in the present time had such excellent taste. The uneven floor was the bare earth, a cold place for the unshod feet of the draw-boy in winter, and under each loom was a hole, into which all "ravellings," or waste threads, were collected. These waste threads were usually a perquisite of the draw-boys, who bartered them for "blackman" and "bools" with some of the half-witted hawkers who frequented the weaving-shops.

Overhead the young visitor would regard with wonder the mysterious beams, shafts, and cords, and all the complicated works of the loom. The threads of the "simple" with their mass of lashes and bridles, at the side of the loom, intruded on the passage, ready for the draw-boy, who was meanwhile playing a game at "bools," or spinning his "peerie" in the street. At meal hours, when he had more time, his favourite sports were shinty and races. There would be an ink-bottle hanging near the weaver's hand, so that he might jot down an argument, or mayhap a verse of rhyme in the midst of his work, and the cage at the window with the imprisoned lark or mavis singing the songs of those delightful woods and braes that were close at hand.

Upstairs was the bright kitchen, with the clean hearth-stone, and "ingle blinkin' bonnily," the well-scoured dishes shining like gold and silver, the peacocks' feathers ornamenting the mantle-piece, and the bookcase in the corner, a thing never absent from the house of the weaver. There was the mother, industrious woman, busy with her wheel, winding the pirns to be sent down in an old hat as soon as the weavers would resume work, and the daughter kenching bridles or tambouring. Nor can ever be for-gotten the feast of bread and cheese then set forth, and the bowl of rich sweet milk (for the mother's folk, in the next street, kept cows), followed by an invitation to go down to the garden.

There at the back of the house, as with nearly all the weavers, was the "yaird," with its turnips and kail stocks getting ready for the joyous time o' Hallowe'en. The draw-boys acknowledged no right of private property in turnips or kail stocks at Hallowe'en time. There were not many fine fruits in these gardens, but always some grand gooseberries—golden sulphurs, or the "big, smooth, green anes," or the "wee, red, hairy anes"—a feast for gods, let alone for boys. But while one might make free with the gooseberries, there were always two or three big bushes of black

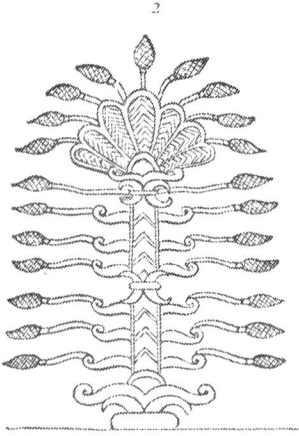

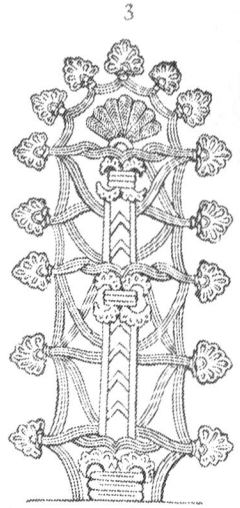

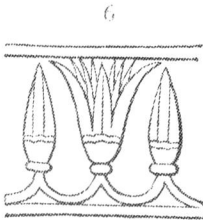

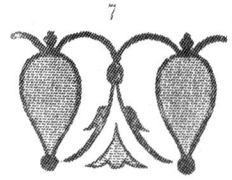

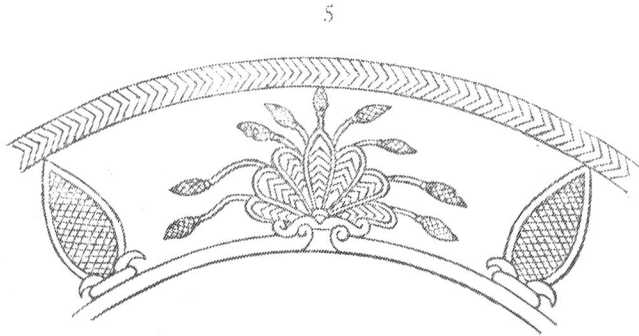

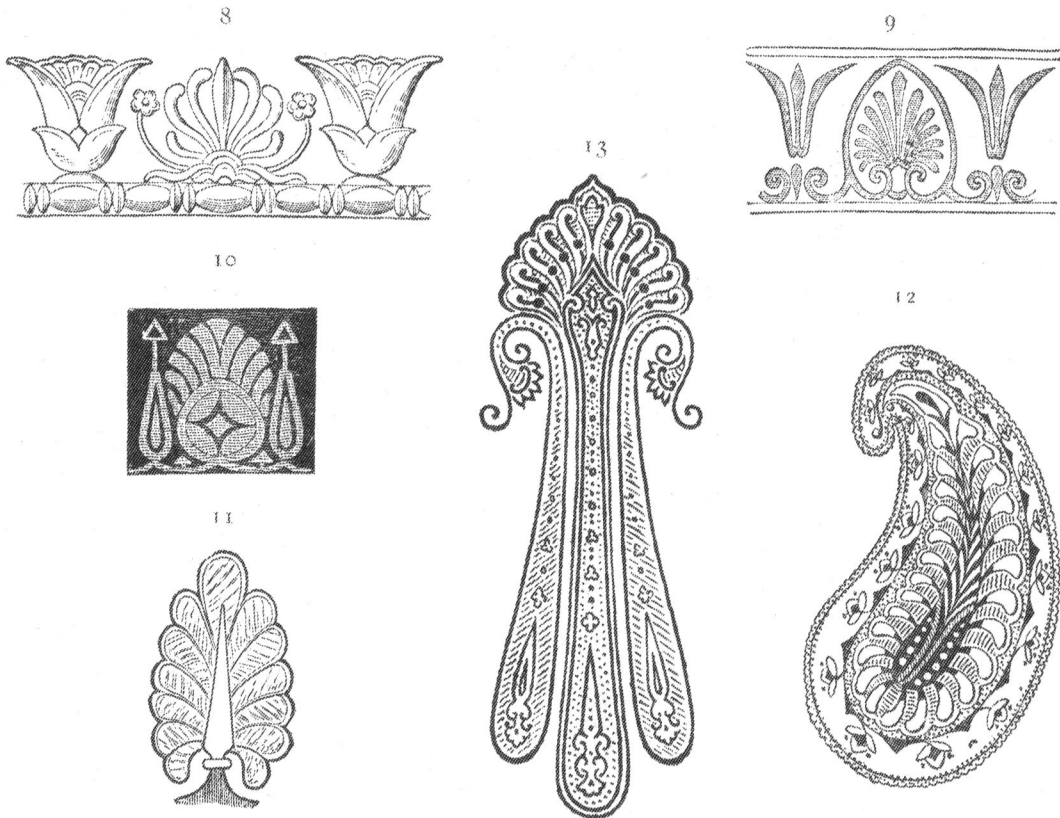

8   9

13

10

12

11

1. The Date Tree throwing off its long-stalked cones.

2. The Soma, the original Hom of the Assyrians, with ~~fan-like head~~ and cones.

3. The Soma, twining about the Date Palm, forming the "Tree of Life," sacred to Asshur, the supreme deity of the Assyrians.

4. The fertilization of the Palm by the artificial transference of the pollen to the clusters of the female or date-bearing tree. The genius holds the cone in his hand, and is in the act of putting it into a palmate at the end of one of the branches.

5. Assyrian breast ornament, showing fan-like head of the Soma and cones alternating with larger representations of the cones.

6. Assyrian knop and flower ornament, based on the lotus and its bud. Though the form is changed, it has still all the significance of the Palm ornament.

7. Indian form of the knop and flower, the cone assuming greater prominence.

8. Indian honeysuckle ornament, Assyrian in origin. The form suggests the Date Tree, but its detail shows it to be a flowering lotus.

9. Greek honeysuckle ornament, probably derived from Assyrian Palm and honeysuckle.

10. Hom-head-like with cone shape between, found in Cashmere and Delhi Shawl borders.

11. Knop and flower combined. The cone looks like the trunk of a tree, and the branches fan out like the fronds of the Hom. Also found in Cashmere and Delhi Shawls.

12. Pine cone section Indian Shawl or fabric. The cone has now become very prominent, and the flowers are used to fill and decorate it.

13. Double Pine taken from a Paisley Shawl. Two upright Pines or cones terminate in scrolls with inflorescence, and a fan-like shape rises between them. It will be observed that the object has all the essential features of the Assyrian Palm and the knop and flower ornament. The general rigidity recalls the severe dignity of the earlier ornament, the Date Tree No. 1, and the Soma No. 2. The trunk has become lengthened cones or pines. The flower is found in the terminal scrolls, as well as in the palmate shape between them, and while this shape suggests the Palm in form, in detail it bears a close resemblance to the honeysuckle ornament No. 8.

(Figures 1 to 11 by permission of the authorities quoted at p. 28.)

currants which were held sacred, and dared not be touched, for these supplied the jam so much in demand for "sair throats" in the coming winter. Then the flowers. No rare or costly blooms, but sturdy, herbaceous Scotch flowers, mostly of strong, aromatic flavour. "Simmer wud," spearmint, and balm; the coarse-smelling tansy, or the more delicately perfumed rosemary or lavender, dear to all thrifty housewives. And then the dusty millers, Highlandman's garters, bachelor's buttons, daisies, flaming orange lillies, and, in the spring, a wealth of yellow daffodils. Of these the visitor would get a "bab" (bouquets were unknown) to be envied by all the children on the way home.

This was the kind of garden that the boys enjoyed and long remembered. Some of the weavers were florists and cultivated to great perfection pansies and roses, but into these gardens the boys had no admission, and, consequently, no sweet memories cluster around them. Some gardens, however, had excellent fruit trees, and it was a not uncommon thing for the "shop" to take a holiday when the fruit was ripe. This they generally did on a Monday. The weavers' part was to shake the trees, while the draw-boys picked up the falling fruit. The boys were rewarded with "pouchfulls," especially of those that the birds had damaged, and had a feast which always made this holiday earnestly desired. The "maisters" usually adjourned to a neighbouring public house for a dram and a debate. Although all this has now passed away, the memory still lingers with delight on these homely scenes.

The Weavers' Union generally arranged once a year for a trip

in the summer time "doon the water," which was looked forward
to with great interest, especially by the boys, who longed to
explore the wonders of the deep.   A delegate in each district sold
the tickets, and draw-boys had them at half-price.   Most frequently
a steamer was hired, to sail from the Sneddon, when the tide
allowed, and after the devious navigation of the Cart to the
"water neb," got joyfully out on the swelling waters of the Clyde,
and made for the Gareloch or Largs, where a happy time was
spent, the boys gathering whelks and "dulse" and hunting for
"partans."   The coming home, however, was occasionally un-
certain and protracted owing to the tide, for high water was
necessary to reach Paisley.   But these adventures only gave the
weavers, and particularly the happy boys, full scope for long
descriptions of the wonders seen and the perils surmounted on the
eventful voyage.

But to return to the draw-boy proper.   Let us try to picture
this terrible urchin as known to Paisley in the days of the harness
weaving.   The draw-boy was so called because he assisted the
weaver at a complicated harness pattern by drawing certain cords
which raised the warp threads, in the way which has since been
more effectually done by the Jacquard machine.   We used to
question if the draw-boys were the sons of the weavers.   We
rather incline to the belief that most of them were "hafflin" herd
laddies sent in to the town by the farmers, as totally unfit to be
broken into any useful work.   They were the terror of Charleston.
Children at play in the street would bolt up a close with their

"bools" and "peeries" whenever the marauding draw-boy appeared. Every widow woman who sold "parleys and black-man," that is, gingerbread and sweetmeats, held them in horror. They knew every orchard in the West End, and what time the gooseberries and apples thereof were ready—for stealing! The sour-milk carts had a bad time of it if ever the milkman left his post, and the passage of the Block Printers' Band would turn out a regiment of tatters which would quite eclipse those which Falstaff marched with through Coventry. They were all advo-cates of the "equal divide," and held fast to the doctrine that "turnips are public property."

The draw-boy was often clad in the cast-off garments of his master, made down to his shape by some unhandy amateur tailor. His carroty head was usually adorned by a blue Kilmarnock bonnet, Once upon a time it had boasted of a red "tourie" on the top, but that had gone long ago, being burnt off and a big hole made by dint of burning "peoys," or masses of damp gun-powder, on his head. Instead of the "tourie," there shot through the bonnet an irrepressible tuft of red hair, like the helmet of Navarre, "still blazing in the van."

Of course every draw-boy kept rabbits and "doos" and white mice or guinea-pigs, and had many a pitched battle over the ownership of these animals. The draw-boy's ideas of "meum et tuum" were rather vague. He believed in—

> "The good old rule, the simple plan,
> That they should take who have the power,
> And they should keep who can."

The quieter draw-boys were sure to have a nest of sparrows, or "spruggies," as they called them in the "shop," which they fed with "drummock," a compound of meal and water, supposed, for some reason, to be specially suitable for these motherless birds.

But when any member of this "harum scarum" fraternity was elevated to the dignity of the "seat tree" as a full-fledged weaver, the transformation was immediate and complete. No politician translated from the stormy arena of the House of Commons to the quiet seclusion of the House of Lords, could ever show a more decided change. Henceforth by him no orchards were robbed, no old wives terrified, no "doos" or rabbits kept. The affairs of the State took possession of his soul. Such terrible questions as "how to pay the National Debt," or "deepen the Cart," absorbed all his energies, so that the minor question of paying his own debts seldom entered his mind. He cherished hopes of being made a Deacon of the Auld Kirk, or a Manager of the West Relief, so that in walk and conversation he became an altered man.

Preliminary Sketch Design

CHAPTER IX

NATIONAL AND LOCAL POLITICS

ALTHOUGH the weavers dealt separately with the manu-
facturers for each piece of work, there were some general
lists of rates to be maintained against the more selfish of the
employers, and hence the Weavers' Trade Union arose. Many a
fierce struggle they had with the manufacturers, more or less
successful. In one of these contests over what was called the
"sma'" shot, they gained a notable victory, which they com-
memorated by instituting a holiday under the name of "Sma'
Shot Saturday." The "sma' shot," as already explained, was a
binding thread not included in the design but necessary for making
a perfect fabric. The masters did not wish to pay for this, but
the weavers stoutly held to their demand and were successful.
This holiday was instituted in 1856 and is still celebrated on the
first Saturday of July, although "sma' shots" are no longer used,
or even understood in Paisley.

Many of the men who began life as weavers rose to be
manufacturers, and also obtained civic distinction in the town.
Politics absorbed much of the weavers' attention. They were all
Reformers in those days and strong Radicals, with even a con-
siderable leaning to Socialism, but always vigorous and intelligent.

It was a common saying that the weavers of the First Ward (the West End) "gave the tone of politics to Europe;" and no doubt some of them believed it, or something near it. Sir Daniel K. Sandford was Member of Parliament for Paisley in 1834, and, on retiring, gave it as his experience that, for Paisley to be adequately represented, there would have to be a Member for every weaver's shop in the town.

The weavers took part in the Radical Movement, which came on after the conclusion of the Napoleonic wars, and was to some extent a consequence of these events. One of their leaders was John Henderson, a cutler to trade, who, it has been said, escaped to America concealed in a herring barrel. It is characteristic that, after the affair blew over, he returned, and subsequently became Provost of the town. Provost Henderson was a Quaker, and a cultured and much-esteemed man, and at one time edited the Paisley section of the *Reformers' Gazette*. He was Provost during the great depression of trade in 1841-2, when the town became bankrupt, and worked hard to alleviate the distress of that unfortunate time.

Some good stories are told of the weavers during the Radical time. They were all "agin the Government" in those days, and at one time a general rising was to take place. One ingenious weaver was reported to have invented a "boo't gun," which was to do great destruction upon the "sogers," while the users were safe. The present generation will have to be told that a "boo't" gun, was a gun that could shoot round a corner!

It is told of another weaver, who kept the roll of the conspirators, that when called upon by his comrades to produce it, confessed that he had burned it, because, said he, " I wis telt that if the sogers fan it on me, they wad chap aff my heid like a sybo," and that although the loss of his head would be no loss to the cause, " it wad be a sair loss tae him." And no doubt it would, yea an irreparable loss.

The " beaming shops" were the great places of meeting for the weavers, when the affairs of the State were to be discussed, and the inevitable " committee with power to add to their number" appointed, which was to carry out the decisions of the meeting. When the weaver gets a web from the manufacturer, it is in the form of a chain, rolled up in a ball. The first process is to spread it properly on a beam. This is done in the beaming shop, and necessitates a considerable clear length of floor. Such a room, lit up by a dozen "crusies," formed the favourite place of meeting. Here were spent many happy nights. Here debate ran high, and burning eloquence was poured forth, and men received a real education, which it is to be feared the present generation of working men can scarcely obtain.

The writer, as a boy, took immense delight if by any chance he could manage to gain access to these weavers' meetings, and now through the mists of years, looks back on these rare occasions as not the least enjoyable and instructive hours of his life. Some of the weavers were good speakers, and could enrich their discourses with appropriate allusions and quotations, especially from the poets, of whom they were particularly fond. Sometimes a less well-informed speaker would get hold of a "lang-nebbit" word which he would introduce so often as to provoke merriment, and have it fastened upon him as a nick-name. Many of these nick-names were very amusing, and not unkindly. One frequent speaker who was accustomed to straighten up a subject, when the discussion got a trifle "ravelled," as was often the case, acquired the name of "Clearhead." Another worthy, not being able to tackle the big word "Constantinople," pronounced it so like "scones-tied-in-a-napkin," that this name stuck to him for the rest of his life.

The comic element and a pawky style of expression that was peculiar to the weavers, were never absent, but were always employed with the utmost good humour. The weavers knew how to conduct public business with decorum, and no rows ever took place. At one meeting an obstinate weaver insisted on keeping his hat on, notwithstanding the protests of the meeting. This was speedily brought to an end by the sarcastie remark, "Let the puir man alane, d'ye no see he has got the scaw?" and off went the hat immediately, as the only way of proving that the owner did not suffer from that disease. This adroit sally was received with roars of laughter.

When the Chartist agitation began, the weavers threw themselves into it with characteristic ardour. The meetings at that time were usually held in the Old Low Church in New Street. Here Daniel O'Connell held forth in 1835, on which occasion that pugnacious divine, the Reverend Patrick Brewster, got into a

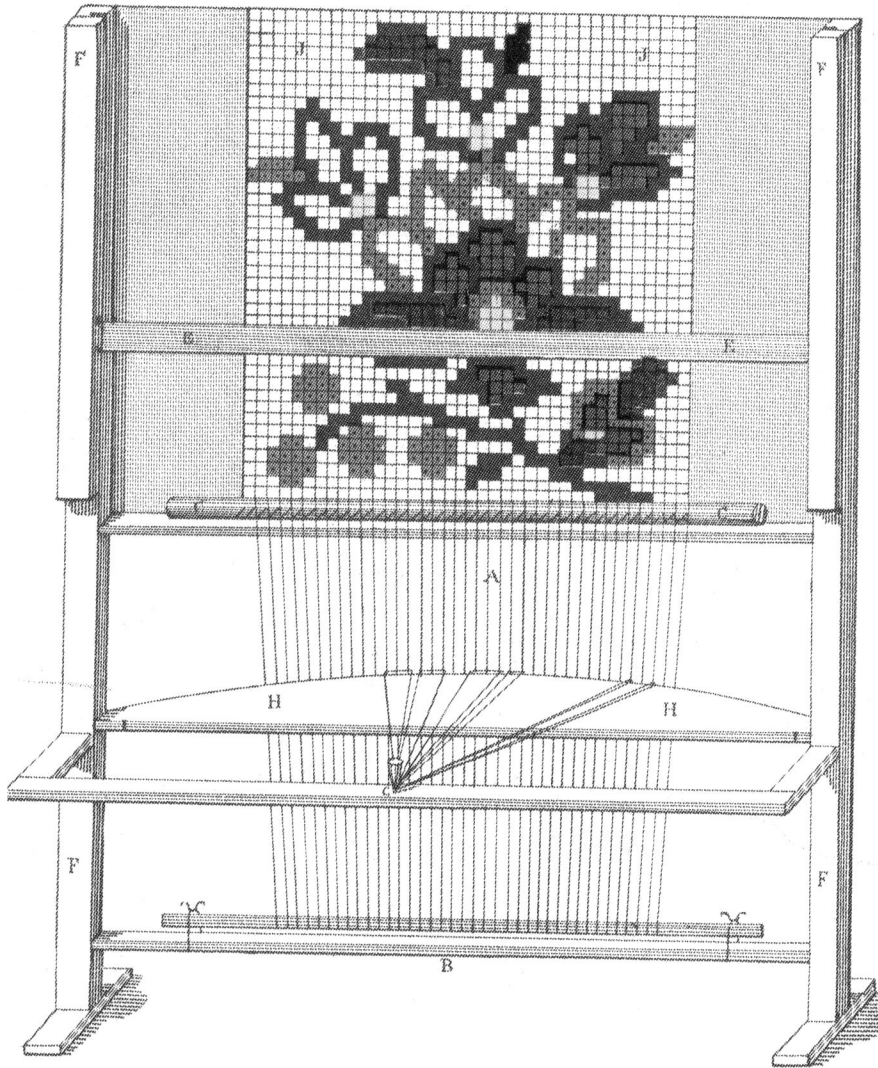

The Lasher's Frame, with design on
point paper

(from Gilroy's "Art of Weaving")

notoriety which lasted through life. Many stirring scenes took place in this hall, which is now classic ground to every old Paisley man.

A leader among the weavers in those days was Robert Cochran. Although more renowned as a speaker than as a weaver, Mr. Cochran, in later life, by the aid of his family, established a thriving drapery trade. He continued to take an active interest in the affairs of the burgh, and after many years of municipal labour, attained the distinction of being Provost of his native town.

In religious matters, also, the weavers had ways of their own. They were in the main a devout and serious class, and much given to theological discussions. Sunday was well observed. The streets were singularly quiet, and the sweet sounds of family worship could be heard in the morning from nearly every house. The staid character of the weavers was not unmixed with a little humour. A weaver of this very solemn and serious order was groaning over a bad web that sorely tried his patience, and was sympathised with by a neighbour, who remarked, "Puir John, ye ken he daurna swear," which would no doubt have relieved his feelings. As was natural, they were nearly all dissenters; indeed, they had a tendency to set up little kirks of their own. This phase of the character of the weavers of Paisley is described with much delightful detail in *The Pen Folk* of the late Mr. David Gilmour. Paisley is fortunate in having had an author, who in such graphic sketches, has immortalized the condition and peculiarities of the harness weavers.

5

CHAPTER X

LITERARY EFFORTS OF THE WEAVERS

THE literary culture which resulted from the conditions of society in the palmy days of the hand-loom weaving, is shown in the number of magazines and periodicals that were started in Paisley. They exhibited considerable merit, but all were very short lived.

The *Weavers' Magazine* was a monthly publication issued in 1818, and twelve numbers only were brought out. It was the only one which had a definite connection with the weaving trade. It gave a monthly review of the various classes of goods then made in Paisley. Many of these were of harness work, with a considerable amount of silk, but the true " Paisley Shawl " had not appeared at that date. There are a few original articles in the magazine, but the greater part consists of instructive and interesting selections, together with a little original poetry of no special note. The names of the authors of original matter are not given.

A more ambitious effort was made in 1828, when the *Paisley Magazine* appeared. It was a monthly publication, and continued for one year. This magazine had no special reference to weavers, but is an indication of the culture of the period. It was got up by a joint stock company, of which the shareholders were :—

66

David Dick, Publisher,	-	-	-	4 shares.
John Neilson, Printer,	-	-	-	3 ,,
William Motherwell, Editor,	-	-	2 ,,
Philip Ramsay, Writer,	-	-	-	2 ,,
John Dunn, ,,	-	-	-	2 ,,
Robert Hay, Clerk to Canal Company,		2 ,,
Dr. George Wylie,	-	-	-	-	2 ,,
William Finlay, Writer,	-	·	-	2 ,,
A. Carlile, Manufacturer,	-	-	-	1 ,,
Andrew Paterson, Writer,	-	-	-	1 ,,

A guinea was advanced for each share. The editor received two guineas for each number issued.

William Motherwell, the poet, who was Sheriff-Clerk Depute at that time, was the editor, and contributed a large part of the contents. Other contributors were Mr. John Dunn, Writer, whose papers show a wide range of reading, and Mr. Robert Hay, Engraver. Mr. Hay had been a sailor in his youth, and besides articles on general subjects, contributed under the *nom de plume*, sometimes of Sam Spritsail, and sometimes of Bill Bobstay, a series of papers which are in a large measure auto-biographical, and much in the style of Smollet's *Roderick Random*.

Although none of the articles are signed, it is known that the following gentlemen, among others, were contributors :—Philip Ramsay, Writer; William Finlay, Writer; A. Carlile, Thomas Crichton, William Kennedy, J. Fullarton, A. Johnston, and

R. Peacock. The descendants of some of these contributors are still among our most respected townsmen. The magazine contains numerous poetical pieces, the greater number being by the editor. The general merit is of a very high order, although the writing would now be considered somewhat heavy. There is no selected matter; all the articles are original.

In 1841 and 1842 appeared *The Renfrewshire Annual*. These two volumes were edited by a lady—Mrs. Maxwell of Brediland—and are only connected with the weaving trade, in so far that all the illustrations in the volume for 1842, except one, are the work of Sir J. Noel Paton, who was a pattern designer in Paisley at that time. They are also the first indication of that graceful drawing of elves and fairies, which the artist carried to great excellence in his later works. Sir Noel, who was plain Neil Paton in those days, was designer to Messrs. Brown, Sharps & Company. (Plate 15).

Another designer at this, or a rather later date, was Alexander Smith, the poet, author of *A Life Drama*, and other works. Smith's father was a designer, and the son was brought up to the same occupation. But he had no special bent for art, and when the shawl trade decayed, he betook himself to the more congenial paths of literature and poetry. His poetical works are of a style of superabundant metaphor much admired at that time. His prose is excellent; his essays particularly so. The scenes in his novel of *Alfred Haggart's Household*, are laid in Paisley and neighbourhood. (Plate 15).

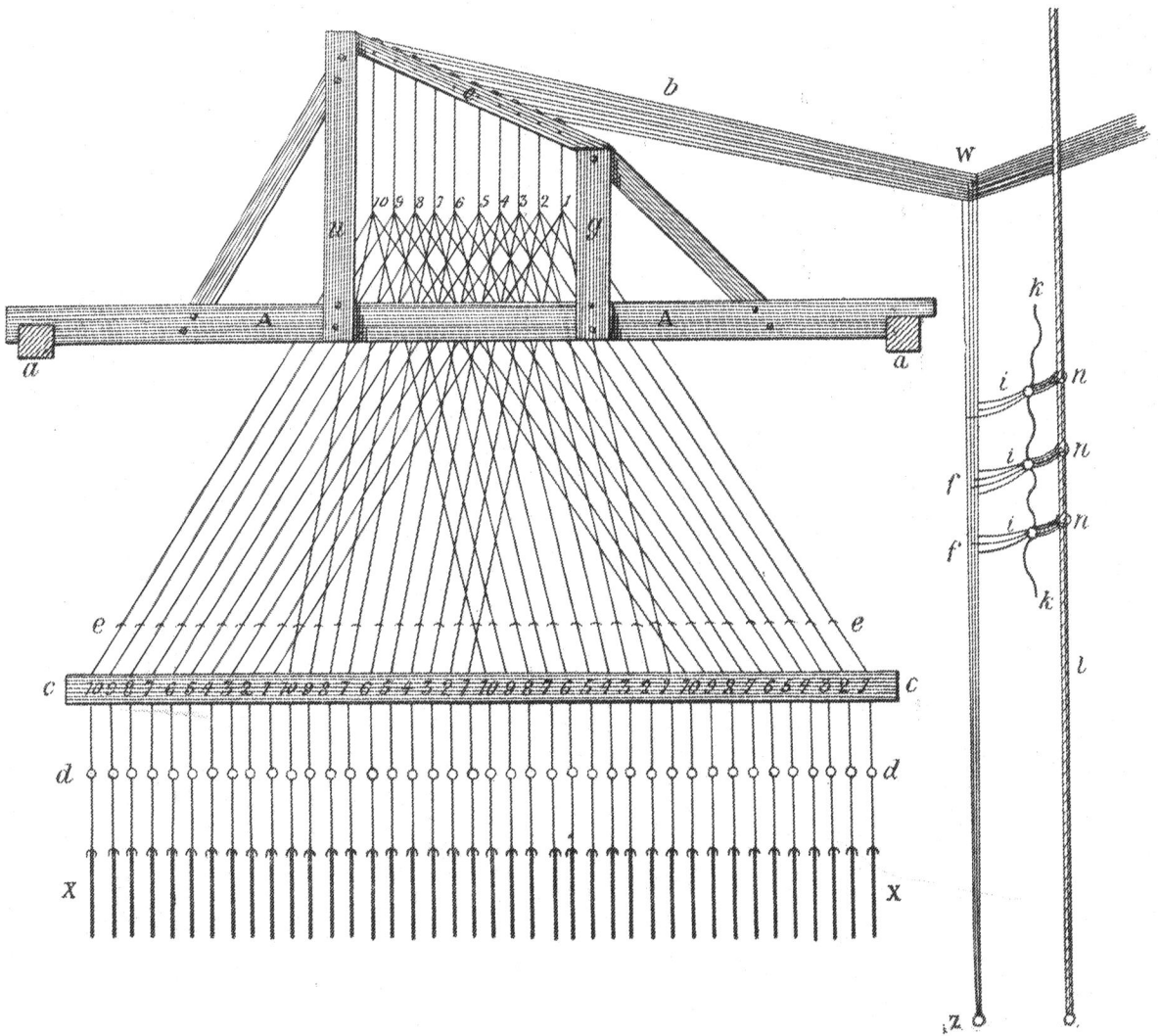

The Draw-Loom

(from Murphy's "Art of Weaving")

Many writers have endeavoured to paint the manners and peculiarities of the Paisley weavers, but none have succeeded so well as the late Mr. David Gilmour, author of *The Pen Folk* and other works. (Plate 15). Although, as he says himself, he never was a weaver, he had worked as a draw-boy and, excepting the mechanical operation of throwing the shuttle, he had learned to understand the loom, as well as most weavers. This early training enabled him to occupy the position of general manager for Mr. Robert Kerr, one of the most prominent of the Paisley Shawl manufacturers, and afterwards to become a manufacturer on his own account. In all these capacities, with so large a part of the weaving population of Paisley passing through his hands, he had wide opportunities of studying and appreciating the weavers' intellectual power and independence of life. Gifted with a natural shrewdness, and a fund of quiet humour, his warm sympathy with the weavers in their difficulties, and his keen sense of justice in dealing with them, brought him very near to them, and made him to be universally beloved. He was a frequent referee in their trade disputes, and that their respect for him was fully reciprocated on his part, he has shown in all his writings. Those who had the pleasure of his acquaintance were always amused by his wealth of anecdote and pawky humour. It is most fortunate that when he saw this type of people and of life passing away for ever, he felt the impulse to record it. He was particularly qualified to appreciate the religious side of the character of the weavers, and this forms the leading note in all his writings.

It was somewhat late in life when, suggested by the death of an old Paisley weaver, Mr. Gilmour sat down to write his charming book, *The Pen Folk*, published in 1871. It was a sketch of the religious side of the Paisley weavers : the story of a little group of earnest Christian men and women, who met every Sunday in a room in the "pen" or passage from High Street to Oakshaw Street. The book gave a delightful picture of the simple manners of the time, and immediately attracted attention. In 1876 he published *Paisley Weavers of Other Days*, where the same subject is continued, but more from the secular side. *Gordon's Loan Sixty Odd Years Ago*, written in 1881, is also a delightful fragment, dealing mostly with the political and socialistic leanings of the weavers, and their longings for the "equal divide."

CHAPTER XI

SOME WELL-KNOWN PAISLEY MEN

THE shawl warehouses were for the most part situated in Causeyside Street, called always *the* Causeyside, and reminiscent, no doubt, of the time when it would be the only street that was paved. The aspect of this street in the palmy days of the shawl trade, in the forenoon of a busy day, was very interesting. The salesmen, always well dressed, might be seen in black surtout coats and shining satin hats, with a flower in the button-hole, lounging at the front doors on the look-out for buyers, expected by the trains from Glasgow. When they did find a customer, they smilingly took him in to inspect their stock, and the transaction among a certain class, often ended by a walk up to " Peter's," for a social glass.

In the intervals of trade, these important individuals had to content themselves with polishing the sides of the front door. Cigars were forbidden, and the era of the cigarette had not yet come. At such times it was rather an ordeal for a Paisley young lady to pass down the Causeyside through a double row of these observing and admiring gentlemen, although it has been recorded that some of them rather relished it. The street was lively with the dyers' little covered vans, taking away or delivering the yarn.

Weavers with round Kilmarnock bonnets might be seen con-
veying away their webs, in clean white linen bags, and numbers
of girls, with shawl over the head, bringing the shawls that they
had been fringing or embroidering.   The harness shawl manu-
facturers gave employment to a great many subsidiary occupations,
and these men were constantly moving about the street, designers,
dyers, croppers, calenderers, finishers, and many others.

We re-produce in Plate 14 portraits of three of the more
prominent shawl manufacturers, out of many that might be named,
did space permit.   Robert Kerr, John Morgan, and David Speirs,
in their various lines, did much to extend the reputation of the
shawl trade, and many of their productions, still carefully
preserved, are among the finest specimens of this class of work.
We have further been enabled by the kindness of Joseph Fulton,
Esq., of Glenfield, to re-produce a photograph of a group of well-
known Paisley men, the greater number of whom were connected
more or less directly with the weaving trade.   (Plate 1.)

It is characteristic of the homely manners of the time, that
these men should have walked out (for cabs were scarce then in
Paisley), to the classic Braes of Gleniffer, two miles south of the
town, on the Queen's Birth Day, Thursday, 29th May, 1856, to
enjoy the hospitality of the genial Laird of the Glen, the late
William Fulton, Esq.   Holidays were few in those days, and this
was no doubt a great occasion.   Photography was in its infancy,
but Mr. Archibald Barr, son of one of the party, had some

ROBERT KERR, 1797--1868

JOHN MORGAN, 1805--1885

DAVID SPEIRS, 1811--1873

Eminent Paisley Shawl Manufacturers

distinction as an amateur photographer, and to this fact we owe this interesting picture.

Mr. Fulton always took a great delight in the society of the old weavers, especially such as were "characters," or who attempted poetry, or at least rhyme, and there was generally a goodly number of both sorts. He would frequently send in his bleachfield carts, and bring out a happy company to spend a pleasant summer day at the Glen, and be regaled with curds and cream. The present group, however, were the "maisters," or "corks," as they were familiarly called. They were all men in active business life; some were men of strong individuality, and the poetical element was not wanting.

The chimney-pot hat was the regular headpiece then for holidays, and was of gigantic dimensions, and generally ornamented with a mourning band, so as to come in handy for funerals, which ornament being kept on for economical reasons, was considered no way out of place on festive occasions. The hat served for a generation, and during that time, as the shape in vogue changed, was certain to be in the height of fashion two or three times. It was the favourite receptacle for loose papers, samples of cloth or yarn, and for those who snuffed, a race long extinct, it carried the inevitable spotted Bandanna handkerchief. It will be observed that all these men are clean shaven. This was the universal custom at the time. Any person wearing a moustache was looked upon as of doubtful character, or as one of those foreigners who came over in such numbers as a consequence of the Revolutions of 1848. But after the return of the troops from the Crimean War, the wearing of the moustache and beard became general. The clergy were brought round by the example set by a popular minister of the Abbey.

The names counting from left to right are :—

1. James Balderston, Thread Manufacturer.
2. John Muir, Warper.
3. John Snodgrass, House Painter.
4. William MacKean, Starch Manufacturer, afterwards Provost.
5. William Fulton, of The Glen.
6. John Hair, Shawl Manufacturer.
7. William Philips, Yarn Merchant, Ex-Provost.
8. James Lang, Leather Merchant, afterwards Bailie.
9. John Neilson, Printer.
10. Bailie William Russell, Dyer, afterwards Town Treasurer.
11. John Smith, Shawl Manufacturer.
12. James Sharp, Manufacturer.
13. John Robertson, of J. & J. Robertson, Shawl Manufacturers.
14. William Anderson, Bookseller.
15. John Macgregor (Poet), Embroiderer, Kilbarchan.
16. William Robb, Manufacturer.
17. James Robertson, of J. & J. Robertson, Shawl Manufacturers,

18. John Barr, Manufacturer.

19. Matthew Tannahill, brother of the Poet. (Seated).

20. George H. Brown, Yarn Merchant. ⎫

21. Robert Fulton, Finisher.   ⎬ (Reclining).

22. Robert Clark, Thread Manufacturer. ⎭

The last-named gentleman is the sole survivor (1903), of this interesting group.

CHAPTER XII

DECAY OF THE SHAWL TRADE.   CONCLUSION

THE Paisley Shawl being an article of luxury and expense, was affected by the vagaries of fashion.   The demand was not constant.   Periods of depression were frequent, and productive of much suffering to the poor weavers.   The history of a new pattern or fabric generally runs a settled course.   At first it is produced of the finest materials, and at a high cost.   It is taken up by the wealthy classes and becomes fashionable.   Soon, however, some manufacturer, desirous of increasing his trade, produces a lower article, and appeals to an extended circle of buyers.   This goes on till the upper classes forsake it for some new attraction, and the trade decays.

The Harness Shawl ran this course.   At one time some of them sold as high as £20.   As long as a demand at this rate endured, the times were prosperous.   But to stimulate demand, lower qualities were made, until the shawl came to be composed entirely of cotton.   The next move was to produce cheap printed imitations.   These efforts only served to throw the true Harness Shawl out of fashion, while the mistaken idea among the weavers, that strikes would mend matters, only accelerated the inevitable end.

76

SIR J. NOEL PATON. 1821--1901

ALEXANDER SMITH, 1829--1867

DAVID GILMOUR, 1811--1889

Notable Paisley Artists and Literary Men

Whatever consequences, some of them not very desirable, the change from hand production to mechanical power, may have brought upon us, it has certainly created a greater and more steady demand for labour. The present generation has little idea of the hard lot which sometimes came, quite unmerited, upon the working-man in past times. In our days poverty is in the main self-made. There is no necessity for it. With a little prudence, industry, and sobriety, qualities which surely every man can possess, no one need despair of attaining to a fair measure of comfort.

But in the days when hand-loom weaving of shawls was the principal, and almost the only industry in Paisley, there were frequent and long-continued times of depression, when even the most frugal and well-behaved operatives had a hard struggle to make ends meet. The "soup kitchens" were a common institution in those days, and often for long periods had to be maintained to keep the poor weavers from absolute starvation. We have now no experience of such a state of matters. It was a misfortune that the town had practically only one form of occupation, and not till more varied industries were established, was this evil mitigated.

Appeals for help were often made. Queen Victoria, always sympathetic with those who were suffering, tried to revive the fashion for Paisley Shawls. But these efforts to bolster up a decaying trade only served to prolong the misery. No patronage of the great could seriously affect the trend of fashion. Business

declined and many firms went into liquidation. The town itself
in 1842 became bankrupt, and only in 1872 was it extricated from
this unfortunate position. Large numbers of the youth of the
town were forced to seek employment elsewhere, and between
1870 and 1880 the manufacture of Harness Shawls ceased
altogether in Paisley.

The subsequent prosperous condition of the town is in a
measure the result of this depression. The male labour having
gone elsewhere, the female labour was quite a drug in the market.
At this time the sewing machine was invented, and came into
extensive use, with the result of creating a great demand for
sewing thread. Thread-making had been long established in
Paisley, and when the increased demand came, the supplying of
it naturally gravitated to where labour was cheap, rather than to
other places where female labour was more expensive. The
Paisley firms had the wisdom to avail themselves of these
economic conditions to extend their business, which has since
gone up by leaps and bounds. In so doing they were conferring
a great benefit on the town, as well as upon themselves. They
brought back a more stable prosperity by establishing an industry
not affected by the uncertainties of fashion, and they have spent
much of their well-earned wealth in adorning and beautifying the
town, while in other and less visible ways, they have exhibited a
princely liberality.

While we view with satisfaction the increased comforts and
advanced prosperity which the town now enjoys, we cannot fail

to note that it is not the old Paisley of the days of the shawl trade. Perhaps no town in the kingdom has undergone such a revolutionary change as Paisley during the last generation. New thoughts, new desires, new methods, absorb the people. The weaving days are almost forgotten. Yet it was in some respects a remarkable past. The period of the Paisley Shawl is a complete epoch. Its life history is ended. It did not evolve into a new form of similar industry; it died absolutely out. It forms, therefore, a subject suitable for an historical sketch; suitable also for being commemorated in the local Museum. A people who take no interest in their glorious past are unworthy of a prosperous present. To all who take pride in their ancient town, this epoch of the Paisley Shawl is a time worthy of being commemorated. No more beautiful and instructive section of the local Museum could be formed, than one which would show some choice specimens representing the marvellous taste and skill of these old harness weavers, with illustrations of the simple machinery with which such results were obtained.

They are gone from us now, this race of fine old men, with their wondrous skill in handicraft, their keen love of nature and of poetry, their sturdy Radicalism, their God-fearing integrity, and their patient suffering in adversity. But it would be well that their memory was kept green amongst us, and that coming generations of Paisley men may be able to regard with pride, the beautiful productions of their forefathers, and learn the lesson, that life need not be a daily uninteresting drudgery, but may be beautified by a loving interest in the products of industry, whatever they may be.   Let the example of these grand old weavers stimulate the workmen of every trade in the town to attain the highest excellence, each in his own department, and to maintain the reputation of the town for artistic taste and high intellectual culture, which was stamped upon it by the old harness weavers. And for this end we commend to the wealthy of the present generation, whose success is directly built upon the decay of the hand-loom industry, to found some enduring record and illustration of the Paisley Shawl.

INDEX

---

www.ingramcontent.com/pod-product-compliance
Lightning Source LLC
Chambersburg PA
CBHW081157270326

41930CB00014B/3191